Great Artists

Jacob Lawrence

ABDO
Publishing Company

Joanne Mattern

**visit us at
www.abdopub.com**

Published by ABDO Publishing Company, 4940 Viking Drive, Edina, Minnesota 55435.
Copyright © 2005 by Abdo Consulting Group, Inc. International copyrights reserved in all
countries. No part of this book may be reproduced in any form without written permission
from the publisher. The Checkerboard Library™ is a trademark and logo of ABDO Publishing
Company.

Printed in the United States.

Cover Photo: Getty Images
Interior Photos: Art Resource pp. 9, 11, 12, 13, 15, 17, 18, 19, 22, 23, 24, 25; Corbis pp. 14, 27;
    Getty Images pp. 1, 5, 21, 29; © 2005 Gwendolyn Knight Lawrence/Artists Rights Society
    (ARS), New York

Series Coordinator: Megan Murphy
Editors: Heidi M. Dahmes, Jennifer R. Krueger
Cover Design: Neil Klinepier
Interior Design: Dave Bullen

Library of Congress Cataloging-in-Publication Data

Mattern, Joanne, 1963-
    Jacob Lawrence / Joanne Mattern.
        p. cm. -- (Great artists)
    Includes index.
    ISBN 1-59197-844-0
    1. Lawrence, Jacob, 1917---Juvenile literature. 2. African American painters--Biography--
Juvenile literature.   I. Title.

ND237.L29M38 2002
759.13--dc22

2004052806

Contents

Jacob Lawrence

Jacob Lawrence was one of the first African-American artists to become popular with both white and black audiences. He created paintings that celebrate African-American heroes. He also recorded the struggles of African Americans moving to the North to find work.

Lawrence spent much of his life in a neighborhood in New York City called Harlem. Harlem was a lively, colorful place. Lawrence created many paintings that showed life in this neighborhood. These works are full of bright colors and movement.

Most of all, Lawrence's paintings celebrate the struggle of all people to survive and flourish. He succeeded in a time when even he didn't believe he could survive as an artist. This accomplishment is still recognized by artists and art lovers in America.

Jacob Lawrence in his
Seattle, Washington, studio

Timeline

1917 ~ Jacob Lawrence was born on September 7.

1930 ~ Lawrence went to live with his mother in Harlem.

1932 ~ Charles Alston started the Harlem Art Workshop.

1934 ~ Lawrence's mother lost her job.

1938 ~ Lawrence began working for the WPA.

1939 ~ Lawrence completed *The Life of Frederick Douglass*.

1940 ~ Lawrence completed *The Life of Harriet Tubman*.

1941 ~ Lawrence and Gwendolyn Knight married; Lawrence finished *The Migration Series*; Lawrence joined the U.S. Coast Guard.

1962 and 1964 ~ Lawrence visited Africa.

1971 ~ Lawrence began teaching art at the University of Washington in Seattle, Washington.

2000 ~ Lawrence died on June 9.

Fun Facts

- Jacob Lawrence once said that he never dreamed he would be a full-time artist. He assumed he would always need to do something else to make a living.

- Charles Alston said of Lawrence, "It would be a mistake to try and teach Jake. He was teaching himself . . . all he needed was encouragement and technical information."

- One of Lawrence's first artistic inspirations was his home in Harlem. His mother always decorated their place, and Lawrence loved the colors and fabrics he saw all around him.

- The Museum of Modern Art in New York bought Lawrence's *The Migration Series*. Lawrence was the first African-American artist to be represented there.

- Today, Lawrence's work is displayed in more than 200 museum collections, including the National Gallery of Art in Washington, D.C.

On the Move

Jacob Lawrence was born in Atlantic City, New Jersey, on September 7, 1917. His parents had moved to Atlantic City from the southern United States. They moved many times to find work.

Jacob's father was also named Jacob. He was a cook for the railroad. Jacob's mother was named Rosa Lee. She cleaned houses for a living. Both parents worked hard to support their children. Jacob had a younger brother named William and a younger sister named Geraldine.

When Jacob was two years old, the Lawrence family moved to Easton, Pennsylvania. His father left the family when Jacob was seven years old. Rosa Lee then took her children to Philadelphia, Pennsylvania, to find more work.

Sometimes Jacob's mother did not have enough money to support her family. So, the children lived with different foster families while Rosa worked in Harlem, New York.

Lawrence enjoyed living in Philadelphia. The city was full of bright colors. He saw red brick houses, green grass, and colorful signs. Later, Lawrence would use these colors, such as in Street Shadows.

Life in Harlem

After saving some money, Rosa Lee finally decided Jacob could live with her. Jacob was 13 years old when he moved to Harlem. He could hardly believe what life was like there.

Harlem was a busy, crowded place. The streets were filled with buildings so tall they seemed to touch the sky. Most of the people who lived in Harlem were poor. But, they were full of energy. Later Jacob said, "There was always a feeling of hope, a feeling of encouragement."

After moving to Harlem, Jacob finished grammar school and began high school. Rosa Lee had to work all day and wanted Jacob to be safe after school. So, she sent him to the Utopia Children's House. Utopia was an African-American community center that offered inexpensive classes.

Jacob went to the Utopia Children's House almost every day. There, his art teacher was a man named Charles Alston. Alston was part of the **Harlem Renaissance**.

Street Scene (Boy with Kite)
is one of Lawrence's many
paintings of city streets.

Alston became Jacob's friend and **mentor**. He taught Jacob how to use paints, pencils, and crayons to draw. Alston also showed Jacob how to sculpt with clay. Jacob loved creating. He later said, "I didn't even realize it was art at the time. I just did it because it was fun."

At the Workshop

In 1932, Alston started the Harlem Art Workshop. The group met at the Schomberg Public Library in Harlem. Alston wanted his students to learn from each other. He encouraged everyone to express themselves.

The goal of the workshop was for each artist to develop his or her own style. Jacob studied how shapes and lines created a picture. He also worked with colors. Jacob learned that he could make powerful pictures with bright colors and simple shapes.

From the beginning, Jacob enjoyed painting the world around him. He painted his family, friends, and street scenes in his Harlem neighborhood.

Lawrence painted the world around him in bright colors.

Harlem Street Scene shows the neighborhood that Lawrence grew to love.

Jacob's Culture

When Jacob was not painting, he was reading or going to museums. He was interested in African-American life. In school, students learned about white history and white heroes. Jacob wondered who the heroes of his African-American **culture** were.

Jacob spent a lot of time studying at the Schomberg Public Library. This library had a large collection of books about African-American history. It also collected African masks and other **artifacts**.

Jacob learned a lot about his culture there. He later used this knowledge in his art to teach other people about African-American heroes.

An African mask like this one inspired Lawrence to learn more about African culture.

Students with Books *shows how important Lawrence thought learning was for African Americans.*

The WPA

In 1934, the country was in the middle of the **Great Depression**. Many people lost their jobs, including Rosa Lee. So, Jacob quit school to earn money. He delivered newspapers, worked in a laundry, and worked at a print shop.

Jacob was working hard. But he made time for art, too. He continued going to the Harlem Art Workshop. The workshop had a new location and a new name. It was now called Studio 306.

Studio 306 received money from a government program called the Works Progress Administration (WPA). The WPA gave money to public projects that employed artists and writers. WPA artists created paintings and sculptures for public places, such as hospitals and post offices.

In 1938, Jacob began working for the WPA. His job was to produce two paintings every six weeks. He was paid about $30 a week. Jacob was thrilled to be paid to paint. Now, he felt like a real artist.

Lawrence wrote the caption,
"They were very poor," for this painting.

African Heroes

After his WPA job, Lawrence began his own projects. He wanted to tell the stories of African heroes through his art. He began a series of paintings about Toussaint-Louverture. Louverture was a slave in the country of Haiti during the 1700s. He organized other slaves and won Haiti's freedom.

Lawrence told the story of Louverture's life in 41 paintings. He hung the paintings in a row. Then, he wrote a **caption** to explain what was happening in each painting. The result was similar to a comic strip. Lawrence called the finished project *The Life of Toussaint L'Ouverture*.

Lawrence continued to tell stories about his heroes through his paintings. In 1939, he completed a series of 32 paintings called *The Life of Frederick*

Part of a panel from **The Life of Toussaint L'Ouverture.** *In 1939, the Baltimore Museum of Art was the first museum to exhibit the series.*

Harriet Tubman leads escaped slaves to freedom in this panel from The Life of Harriet Tubman.

Douglass. Douglass was an escaped slave who became a famous speaker and writer.

The next year, Lawrence completed 31 paintings called *The Life of Harriet Tubman*. Like Douglass, Tubman was an escaped slave. She led many other slaves to freedom. All of these paintings used simple shapes and bright colors to tell the stories of African-American heroes.

Critical Praise

Lawrence's work got a lot of attention in the art world. Several important newspapers and magazines wrote about him. Both black and white **critics** liked his work. A magazine called *Opportunity* even said Lawrence was a genius!

Lawrence was pleased that people enjoyed his art. But he would have painted even if no one did. Lawrence painted because he liked to. He felt that the work itself was its own reward.

In 1940, Lawrence received money from the Julius Rosenwald Fund. This award was created to improve the education of African Americans. Lawrence won the award twice more. The money allowed him to rent his own studio. Now, he could start working on a larger project.

After succeeding with his paintings of African-American heroes, Lawrence continued to exhibit his work in galleries.

Great Migration

Lawrence wanted to tell the story of his own family and others like his. Since about 1916, African-American families had been **migrating** from the southern United States to the North. These families looked for better jobs and more equal treatment.

This huge movement of people became known as the Great Migration. Lawrence's parents had been part of this. So had many of his neighbors and friends. Lawrence wanted to tell their stories in a huge project called *The Migration Series*. He started working on it in 1940.

Sixty paintings make up *The Migration Series*. Lawrence wanted all the paintings to look similar. So, he laid the paintings out

Members of the Great Migration travel in **The Migration Series.**

and worked on all of them, one color at a time. He also added **captions** to each painting.

*The **Migration** Series* shows how African Americans traveled north to find work. It explains in pictures and words their hopes and fears. And, it shows the triumphs and the disappointments of life in the North.

A train crowded with migrants on their long journey to the North

Love and Success

An artist named Gwendolyn Knight helped Lawrence create *The **Migration** Series*. Knight and Lawrence met at Studio 306. They spent a lot of time together. In 1941, they married.

That year, Lawrence finished *The Migration Series*. He showed the work to Edith Halpert, a New York art dealer. Halpert showed *The Migration Series* at her gallery. It was the first time her gallery showed the work of an African-American artist.

The Migration Series received a lot of attention. Lawrence's work was praised and honored. *Fortune* magazine printed 26 of the paintings with a special article on African Americans.

Many of Lawrence's paintings represent the jobs of African Americans, such as working on the railroad.

Artist's Corner

Many of Lawrence's creations, including *The Migration Series*, were made of tempera on hardboard. Tempera is paint that uses something other than oil, such as egg yolk, to mix with dye. Hardboard is an inexpensive, smooth material.

Most of Lawrence's materials were simple. In fact, he began his painting career by illustrating street scenes on cardboard! One of his favorite mediums was gouache. This was watercolors mixed with a kind of gum. It created a shiny surface on the canvas.

Even Lawrence's simple paintings are powerful. He began the caption for the painting on the left with, "Industries boarded their workers in unhealthy quarters." The caption for the painting on the right is, "Housing was a serious problem."

A Difficult Time

In 1941, the United States entered **World War II**. Lawrence joined the U.S. Coast Guard, which was then a part of the navy. As an African American, Lawrence had few job options. So, he worked serving the officers.

While in the Coast Guard, Lawrence was still allowed to create art. In fact, part of his job included painting pictures of Coast Guard life. He later had a full-time job as an artist for the Coast Guard.

World War II ended in 1945. Lawrence went back to Harlem. He was then invited to teach at Black Mountain College in North Carolina. This was the first of several teaching positions Lawrence would hold.

Although he continued working, Lawrence was unhappy. His art was popular, but other black artists could not succeed. Lawrence struggled to understand why success was so hard for some.

So, Lawrence went to a **psychiatric** hospital for help with his depression. During his nine months in the hospital, Lawrence painted many of the patients. Once again, he used his talent to show how people lived.

Lawrence (far left) *hangs out with his Coast Guard buddies.*

Teaching Others

Lawrence continued painting after he left the hospital. He painted African Americans fighting to win equality. Lawrence also visited Africa in 1962 and 1964. He experienced African **culture** firsthand and showed his work.

But, Lawrence did not want to be known as just an African-American artist. He wanted people to appreciate his art. He did not want people to like it just because he was African American.

Lawrence enjoyed teaching his craft to others. He remembered how Alston and other teachers had guided him when he was a young artist. In 1971, the University of Washington in Seattle invited Lawrence to teach art.

The Lawrences were not sure if they wanted to leave New York City. But they decided they were ready for a change. So, they moved to Seattle. Lawrence continued to paint while in his new home.

Lawrence continued telling stories through art. In 1986, he retired from teaching. Jacob Lawrence died on June 9, 2000. Today, he is remembered as an artist, a storyteller, and a teacher.

Lawrence at a showing of his work in Seattle, Washington, in 1986

Glossary

artifact - a useful object made by human skill a long time ago.

caption - a written description of a cartoon or photograph.

critic - a professional who gives his or her opinion on art or performances.

culture - the customs, arts, and tools of a nation or people at a certain time.

Great Depression - a period (from 1929 to 1942) of worldwide economic trouble when there was little buying or selling, and many people could not find work.

Harlem Renaissance - a time during the 1920s and 1930s when African-American artists, writers, and musicians gathered in Harlem, New York.

mentor - a guide who serves as a good example.

migrate - to move from one place to another.

psychiatry - a branch of medicine that diagnoses and treats mental illnesses.

World War II - from 1939 to 1945, fought in Europe, Asia, and Africa. Great Britain, France, the United States, the Soviet Union, and their allies were on one side. Germany, Italy, Japan, and their allies were on the other side.

Saying It

psychiatric - seye-kee-A-trihk
Renaissance - reh-nuh-SAHNS
Toussaint-Louverture - TOO-SAN-LOO-VEHR-TOOR
Utopia - yoo-TOH-pee-uh

Web Sites

To learn more about Jacob Lawrence, visit ABDO Publishing Company on the World Wide Web at **www.abdopub.com**. Web sites about Lawrence are featured on our Book Links page. These links are routinely monitored and updated to provide the most current information available.

Index